COMMITTED TO CHRIST

40 DEVOTIONS FOR A GENEROUS LIFE

COMMITTED TO CHRIST:
SIX STEPS TO A GENEROUS LIFE

Program Guide With CD ROM

Lays out the basic plans for the campaign, including schedules, team roles, sermon illustrations, worship helps, letters, and commitment cards. Art, files, schedules, and task lists are found on the accompanying CD-ROM.
978-1-4267-4351-1

Adult Readings and Study Book

Designed for use in the six-week small group study that undergirds the program, as well as by others participating in the program.
978-1-4267-4352-8

Small Group Leader Guide

Contains everything a leader needs to organize and run a small group or Sunday school class in support of the program, including discussion questions, activities, and flexible session lengths and formats.
978-1-4267-4353-5

Devotional Book: 40 Devotions for a Generous Life

Devotional companion for program participants. Each of the forty devotions includes Scripture, a brief story or meditation, and a prayer.
978-1-4267-5488-3

DVD: Worship Videos

Designed for the worship experience, this DVD contains seven pre-worship gathering time loops and seven lead-ins.
843504026929

CD-ROM: Tweets, Posts, and Prayers

Contains devotions and prayers for use during the program to build interest and excitement using social media: texts, Twitter, blogs, and email.
843504027681

Preview Book: Six Steps to a Generous Life

A pocket-sized book designed to introduce the congregation to the themes of the six-week Committed to Christ experience.
978-1-4267-4690-1

Committed to Christ Kit

One of each component. 843504028886

BOB CROSSMAN

COMMITTED TO CHRIST

40 Devotions for a Generous Life

by Ben Simpson

ABINGDON PRESS
Nashville

COMMITTED TO CHRIST
40 DEVOTIONS FOR A GENEROUS LIFE
by Ben Simpson

Based on an original work by Bob Crossman

Copyright © 2012 by Abingdon Press
All rights reserved.

This book is printed on acid-free, elemental chlorine-free paper.

ISBN 978-1-4267-5488-3

Library of Congress Cataloging-in-Publication applied for.

12 13 14 15 16 17 18 19 20 21—10 9 8 7 6 5 4 3 2 1

MANUFACTURED IN THE UNITED STATES OF AMERICA

Contents

Contents

Contents

Introduction

Christian life at its best is marked by generosity. Followers of Jesus should be eager to serve. They should abound in charity, love, hope, and faith. Christians should be like their Master. Jesus himself said in Luke 6:40, "Disciples aren't greater than their teacher, but whoever is fully prepared will be like their teacher." Those committed to Christ are called to be like Christ. They are called to live a generous life.

Often, when we think of generosity our first association is financial giving. Christian generosity certainly includes financial giving as a key feature but also transcends it, reaching beyond provision of funds for the poor and for worthy causes, and taking hold of every aspect of our character. But again, as Jesus says, we must be "fully prepared" to be like our teacher. Generosity is a virtue that must be learned. Even those of us who are naturally inclined to give can grow in this grace through the contemplation and application of Christian truth.

If you desire to lead a generous life, recognize that there is a deep need for transformation. Sin must be put to death, and grace must be put on display. God must enact change in you, and you must be willing to receive God's loving discipline. Your kingdom must be subsumed within Christ's Kingdom. There must be a new rule, and a new Lord. Everything you have is no longer yours but has been bought with a price. Through Christ, you have been freed from sin and made alive to God, to be used for his purposes in the world.

My friend and mentor, James Bryan Smith, powerfully describes the implications of this transformation, writing:

> Our little kingdoms are not our own. We are stewards of God's gifts; everything belongs to God. That changes everything. No longer can I say, "What is mine is mine to do with what I please." Instead, "What is mine is not really mine, but God's," and therefore I must ask, "How shall I use the gifts you have given me?" This fundamental shift affects all our daily decisions.[1]

Once the deep realization of Christ's Lordship takes hold in your life, generosity will ensue. How you use your gifts, talents, finances, time, and more will be recast in a new light. And once you truly begin to see the scope and the power of Christ's calling, you will be changed.

How to Use This Book

This devotional guide was written to accompany Commitment to Christ: Six Steps to a Generous Life, by Bob Crossman.

Based upon Bob Crossman's six steps, these reflections are intended to help the reader grow in Christian maturity through prayer, Bible reading, worship, witness, financial giving, and service. These "holy habits" help us to grow as followers of Jesus. As we grow, we begin to evidence the fruit of the Spirit: love, joy, peace, patience, kindness, gentleness, and self-control, as well as abounding in love and charity. Drawing near to Christ, as we shall see, leads to a generous life.

I recommend reading one devotional entry each day. Carry what you discover with you as you go about your daily tasks. The meditations following each Scripture selection illuminate the meaning through illustration or theological exploration, and the written prayers assist you in connecting with God. If you fall behind or miss a day, do not be discouraged. Let the words of the Desert Fathers, a group of fourth and fifth century Egyptian monks, guide you: "Abba Poemen said about Abba Pior that every single day he made a fresh beginning."[2] If you stumble in discipline, accept God's grace and begin again.

At the end of each theme, before beginning the next, you'll find a brief but important section called "Taking a Step." In this section you are invited to move from being to doing, from meditation to discernment and thoughtful commitment. As you consider the questions and challenges in this section, feel free to jot down your thoughts and plans in the margins.

A final word concerning the use of this book: though written to accompany Commitment to Christ, it can be used independently. Anyone seeking God will benefit from the practice of guided Scripture reading, meditation, and prayer. It is my prayer that these reflections will help you to connect with God, and in so doing they will assist you in attaining Christian maturity.

Join the Dance of the Generous God

As Christians we serve an incredibly generous God, yet we are not always as generous as we might be. We fall prey to the temptation to be self-centered rather than other-focused. How can we change this? One answer lies in a deeper understanding of the Trinity. Once we look upon God as Trinity, what alternative do we find? Presbyterian minister Timothy Keller says it well:

> Instead of self-centeredness, the Father, the Son, and the Spirit are characterized in their very essence by mutually self-giving love. No person in the Trinity insists that the others revolve around him; rather each of them voluntarily circles and orbits around the others.[3]

Did you catch that? The God whom Christians worship is "characterized . . . by mutually self-giving love." God is generous, even within God-self. The Father, Son, and Holy Spirit each give of themselves to please and serve one another in an infinite dance of infinite delight. And we are invited to join the dance. This invitation comes through Jesus Christ.

As we learn the rhythms of grace, we too become generous. We increasingly come to reflect the reality of the God that we worship, who endlessly pours forth grace.

May you grow in your depth of commitment to Jesus Christ through these readings, and through that relationship may you come to realize fully the riches you already possess in Christ, generously sharing with all what you have received. May you abound in generosity, evidenced in every dimension of your life. May your abounding generosity embody for others the presence and love of God the Father, Son, and Holy Spirit, so that you may give faithful witness to his truth among your fellow Christian travelers and before the watching world.

An Invitation to Follow

1. THE INVITATION

"Come, follow me."
Mark 1:17

I can remember, as a boy, sitting along the shore of Lake Tyler in Texas, listening to the story of Jesus, attentive and aware that the words I was hearing could have great consequence for my life. I was given a choice, an invitation. I was told that Jesus had called men and women to follow him, and that the invitation still stands today.

Knowingly or not, all of us follow someone. We can do so with great intention and care, or we can do so haphazardly, stumbling from here to there but nevertheless moving in a general direction. We identify those persons whom we most desire to emulate, and we make our decisions accordingly. We all have some general conception of what the good life looks like, either through exposure to a model or by piecing together a patchwork ideal all our own. It remains with us to discern whether or not our focus will be on Jesus as our model, or on something or someone altogether different.

Dallas Willard, author and professor of philosophy at USC, once relayed the story of an encounter with a student who approached him, incredulous, after discovering Willard was a Christian.[4] Willard said, "Yes, I follow Jesus. Who else would you recommend?" Willard contends there is no one more worthy of our discipleship and devotion than Jesus. And if this is true, answering Jesus' call to follow is the wisest and most worthwhile decision we could ever make.

As you begin this journey toward living a more generous life, your first step is Jesus Christ. You must consider his invitation, his life, his path, his truth. You must ask whether you are ready to accept Jesus as worthy of your devotion, your dedication, your wholehearted discipleship.

God has supplied you with the grace necessary to consider what a life committed to Christ entails. Trust him, whether for the first time or yet again. Turn your life over to him, and see what good and beautiful things he might bring.

Lord Jesus, I have heard your invitation to follow you. Give me the grace to respond faithfully, with a committed heart, a renewed mind, and willing hands. I wish to be your disciple, and I trust you to lead me in a good way, a way that leads to a generous and beautiful life. In your name, Amen.

2. GOD'S UNPARALLELED LOVE

We love because God first loved us.
1 John 4:19

Before you made any move toward God, before you discovered or contemplated or considered Jesus's invitation to follow him, God moved toward you. Before you did or said anything, God declared a deep, abiding love for you. This is a life-altering truth.

Our capacity for love is influenced significantly by the love we have received. If our parents and other adults have loved us well throughout our lives, we find it easier to pass along love and encouragement to others.

But unfortunately, not all of us have this experience. There are those of us who have not received love and encouragement from others. The result is a deep wound.

Where human beings have failed us, God remains steadfast. Having experienced the wounds this world has to offer, unparalleled love awaits discovery, made manifestly real in the person of Jesus Christ, who himself was wounded on the cross, proving the depth of his love for you.

Once you grasp that, once you really see it, you will be transformed. A desire to follow will be close behind. The Cross has overcome any deficit of love, any wound you have received. Thus, Jesus's invitation to follow him is not only comprised of doing what he commands (though it is certainly that as well), but is an invitation to a deep and everlasting communion of love.

Following Jesus is a natural consequence of a deep realization of who he is. John Wesley, who at Aldersgate saw that "Christ died for me, even me," is but one example of the transformative power of beholding the depth of God's love displayed on the Cross.

Likewise, may you behold God's love and, as a follower of Christ, demonstrate that love to others.

Lord, help me to hear your call and follow you as a deep expression of love, a love that is to be cherished and delighted in, deeper than any love I have yet to experience. Let this love wash over me and heal me and fill me up, so that I might be poured out in service to the world, following the pattern of your Son, Jesus. May my commitment to you be a response to your deep love and commitment to me, to save me, to redeem me, and to use me for your purposes. Amen.

3. THE MASTER'S VOICE

"So, now, revere the Lord. Serve him honestly and faithfully.
Put aside the gods that your ancestors served beyond
the Euphrates and in Egypt and serve the Lord."
Joshua 24:14

Miss Elizabeth was a coworker of mine, very passionate about children and about Jesus. She constantly dreamed about ways of teaching others clearly and persuasively the truths of the Christian faith.

One day, she told me the story of a man she had encountered who visited prisoners with a dog that had been trained to obey his commands. On the man's visits, he would call out numerous commands, and the dog would obediently respond. These commands ranged from the commonplace, such as sit and stay, to the advanced, such as speak, retrieve certain objects, and more.

At one point during his presentation, the man encouraged prisoners to call out commands. He even allowed the prisoners to use various enticements, such as treats. But the dog would not respond to any other voice. He would not listen or move for anyone but his master.

The man drove this point home, saying that human beings, too, have a master. We are created for God, to be used for his purposes, if we would only listen. But we give in to enticements and other voices, and we serve other gods. When we do this, we often tread a path of destruction, leaving in our wake broken hearts, broken lives, disappointments, and failures.

The call to follow Jesus is an invitation to choose him as our master, as the one who always knows what is best for us, and who trains and equips us to follow all his commands. Christ is calling you to follow him, to serve him, and to be transformed by him. God will take your talents, abilities, passions, and unique personality and use it for the good.

Turn your life over to Jesus. Leave behind old gods and embrace him as Lord.

Almighty God, help me choose to serve you this day rather than gods of wealth, beauty, or power that I may have chosen in former times. In you alone will I find life, both now and everlasting, and I know that by trusting my soul to your loving care you will transform me into a new creature, one who desires to serve and honor you with my time, treasure, and talents. Amen.

4. STEP FORWARD

"Be very brave and strong as you carefully obey all of the
instruction that Moses my servant commanded you.
Don't deviate even a bit from it, either to the right or left.
Then you will have success wherever you go."
Joshua 1:7

For several summers I served as a leader at a United
Methodist camp that has a long history of helping teenagers grow
as followers of Christ. Each summer the students were offered
an opportunity to participate in a trust walk. The students would
be blindfolded and, along with a student or adult guide, would
navigate by the guide's voice or by a hand gently placed upon a
shoulder. The students were fully reliant on their guide. If they
let go, they might find themselves in danger. If they didn't listen,
they might fall or bump into an obstacle.

In Joshua 1:7, God spoke to Joshua prior to Israel's entry
into the land shortly following the death of Moses. Joshua was
afraid. He was stepping into the shoes of a man who had spoken
with God face to face, as a friend. The task before Joshua was
tremendous. The people expected him to lead them as they
fought for the land.

As you commit your life to Christ, you may find the task before you intimidating. You may be scared. It is daunting to imagine yourself becoming a different person. The battles you will face ahead may appear threatening.

But, like the women and men in the Bible, God calls you to pay attention to the Scriptures and the teachings of trusted pastors, teachers, and godly examples. As you move forward, you are not alone. God promises to journey with you. He says to you, as he told Joshua, "Be very brave and strong."

When you feel blindfolded, when you are unsure of the next step, God will be there to guide you. Listen for the divine voice. Over the coming weeks, through prayer, Bible reading, worship, witness, financial giving, and service, your ability to hear God's voice will be sharpened. As you come to greater clarity concerning God's voice, you are invited to step forward in obedience, doing what Jesus calls you to do.

Gracious God, help me to follow your path, deviating neither to the right nor the left. Give me the grace required for the journey, that I may be very brave and strong. Amen.

TAKING A STEP

Have you made a firm commitment to follow Jesus Christ?

If so, evaluate your commitment. If not, do so today.

Speak with a pastor or trusted friend for wisdom, guidance, and encouragement.

Prayer

5. PETITIONS TO A GENEROUS GOD

*"I will do whatever you ask for in my name, so that the
Father can be glorified in the Son. When you ask
me for anything in my name, I will do it."*
John 14:13-14

Imagine staying at a prestigious hotel as a personal guest of
the owner. The owner is a good, gracious, and humble person. At
the beginning of your stay, the owner instructs the concierge to
grant your every request. Extra towels, special services, extravagant food, transportation, and access to any portion of the hotel
will be granted.

These requests may require extra effort, but they fall within
an acceptable range of services the concierge expects to offer in
light of the generous character of the owner.

But what if you abused your status as a privileged guest? Imagine if you wrote graffiti on the walls or threw a television set from a high balcony. Would the concierge continue granting your requests, or would he deny them based on the character of the owner, knowing such acts would bring him disgrace?

In today's Scripture, there is a subtle point contained in Jesus' words, one that could easily be missed. It is not simply a matter of our asking Jesus for anything we desire in order to benefit ourselves. Jesus says he acts on our behalf "so that the Father can be glorified in the Son."

Jesus acts to bring glory to God the Father through the granting of our requests. Therefore, the requests made in his name must take a certain shape, they must be "in Christ," reflecting the character and heart of the one who declares he will grant us "anything."

Just as the Son continually seeks to glorify the Father, when we find ourselves in Christ, we bring our petitions to him in accordance with his very character so that in us, glory might be brought to the Father. We must remember this when we speak with God.

When you pray, ask God for anything, but remember God's character. Ask that your soul might be formed in Christ-likeness. Then, as you grow, your petitions will become more and more glorifying to God, for they will reflect the heart of the one you both follow and worship.

Father, teach me to pray in a way that will bring you glory. Form Christ in me, so that my heart will become like his heart. Amen.

6. WRONG INTENTIONS

You ask and don't have because you ask with evil intentions,
to waste it on your own cravings.
James 4:3

Does God always give us what we ask for? Of course not. Good thing, too!

But why? God gives us permission to ask for anything. Yet we do not always receive what we ask for, sometimes to our great disappointment. The book of James gives us one reason why we may not receive what we ask for: we do not ask with a right heart, and therefore God's "no" is justified. Rather than sulking, we must learn.

Think of the relationship between a parent and child. If the parent grants every request the child makes, the child never matures or grows. Children ask for cotton candy until they are sick, but the loving parent will deny the request before that moment comes.

Likewise, adults often desire the very things that bring about their destruction: money, sex, and power top the list. God, in ultimate wisdom, does not always give us what we ask. And we should be thankful. Learning to pray entails learning to humbly accept when the answer is no. Not everything we ask for, if granted, would be to God's glory or our benefit.

W. H. Auden wrote, "Evil is unspectacular and always human, and shares our bed and eats at our own table."[5] The evil that resides in our hearts is not always easy to discern. This is all the more reason to pray. Through prayer we open our hearts to God and create space for the Holy Spirit, who brings to consciousness our need for repentance and a renewed reliance on God's grace.

Before you become too discouraged, remember that it is God's desire to remake you in the image of Jesus. God sincerely desires to remove from you every evil impulse, and a day is coming when he will bring that work to completion.

Gracious God, teach me to accept humbly those moments when you say no to my request. Let me regard those occasions as an opportunity to examine my heart and discover an evil desire or a wrong intention, if this is the reason you have denied my request. By your Holy Spirit, give me a new heart that brings honorable requests before you. Amen.

7. THINGS WE HAVE NOT KNOWN

The Lord proclaims, the Lord who made the earth, who formed and established it, whose name is the Lord; call to me and I will answer and reveal to you wondrous secrets you haven't known.
Jeremiah 33:2-3

You have been claimed by God in Christ. You are a child of God. God, "the Lord who made the earth," invites you to bring your questions and your thoughts, both great and small, and come before the throne. God then says you will receive an answer. You will be taught. You will discover things you have not known.

James Sire, a Christian thinker and author, once told the story of hearing a respected philosopher speak to a gathering of Christian leaders, all of whom were dedicated to intellectual aspects of the faith. He challenged them to consider the words that most readily came to mind when they thought of Jesus, and asked if those in attendance thought of Jesus as "smart." Did these intellectuals consider Jesus to be foremost among the greatest thinkers who had ever lived? Did these intellectuals think of Jesus as a source that could be trusted in all things? And did these intellectuals, when seeking knowledge, ask Jesus for his counsel, guidance, and assistance in plumbing the depths of difficult intellectual questions?

Sire, along with his colleagues, was flabbergasted. In their pursuit of knowledge, they had failed to consider Jesus as their greatest resource.[6]

Often, we think of God as the one who grants our requests: our divine waiter or cosmic vending machine. We forget that God is also the One who made all that is, and in whom is found all true knowledge and wisdom. God desires to teach us.

Whatever your pursuit, you may bring it before God in prayer. You may ask to receive knowledge, to be instructed. Jesus, as your teacher, will instruct you. As his disciple, he will "reveal to you wondrous secrets you haven't known." There is no question too great for him; no matter outside the purview of his glorious wisdom and knowledge.

After all, he is the Lord of all.

Eternal God, help me to trust you as the source of all knowledge and wisdom, and to bring before you my questions, my concerns, my every thought. Teach me according to what is true, and reveal things to me that I have not known. Amen.

8. Take It to the Lord in Prayer

Do not be anxious about anything; rather bring up all of your
requests to God in prayers and petitions, along with giving thanks.
Philippians 4:6 ♀ 7

What are you most anxious about? Do you struggle to pay the bills? Is your marriage in crisis? Are you stuck in a dead-end job? Do you have friendships that are under strain?

Life is not easy. We are burdened by the concerns of the commonplace, the small yet continual concerns that come from being in relationship with other people or from dealing with the responsibilities of the workplace or school. We also are burdened with greater concerns—causes that capture our hearts, stories of a developing movement, hotly debated issues in the political or ecclesial realms, and more.

We live in a stress-filled time, plagued by busyness and pressure and worry. But we are encouraged to take our anxieties to God in prayer.

In today's Scripture, Paul differentiates between petitions and giving thanks. In prayer, we do both. We bring our requests before God, but we also offer thanksgiving for those things we have received.

It may be helpful for you to write down your prayers and petitions, as well as those things for which you are thankful. Then, you can return to them again and again, praying for certain things with regularity. You will be reminded of those things and can periodically check progress and gain awareness of exactly what God has done. As my friend James Bryan Smith has observed, we often forget how many prayers God has answered, for we do not write them down so that we might remember.[7] But if we did write these things down, oh, the praises we might then offer!

God of all comfort, I bring my worries and anxieties to you, for in you I find rest. I trust that you hear my petitions and that you also hear those things for which I can give you thanks. Not only do I find relief from stress by entering into your presence, I also find a reason for rejoicing, for I have received blessings from your hand. By the Spirit, may I be reminded this day of the many things I can be thankful for, while also turning over every stress, worry, or anxiety that falls heavy upon my heart to your loving and eternal care. Amen.

9. Consider Your Posture

Let my prayer stand before you like incense;
let my uplifted hands be like the evening offering.
Psalm 141:2

Prayer often has an accompanying posture. Let us contemplate this. How were you taught to pray? My daughter has learned to hold hands and to close her eyes when we bless our meals together at home. In Sunday school, she has learned to clasp her hands in front of her, to bow her head, and to close her eyes while led in prayer. She has learned postures to accompany her prayer. The petitions of the psalmist rise before God, accompanied by uplifted hands.

I can remember the first time I was encouraged to be mindful of God's presence with my thoughts, my words, and my posture. I learned that what I do with my body while entering the presence of God in prayer—whether it be with palms upturned toward heaven, a hand raised in praise, my body face down and cruciform before God's throne, or in a simple kneeling posture—can deepen my expression and complement the words I wish to speak.

Take a moment to focus on a particular concern you need to bring before God. If you need to confess your sin and offer repentance, you may wish to lay face down on the floor in a posture of humility and contrition. If you need to offer thanks, you may wish to raise your hands high in celebration. If you need to receive grace, you may want to extend an open hand, asking God to fill your palm with grace overflowing.

Consider your body posture during prayer. Do you sit still in a comfortable chair? Do you kneel beside your bed or in another place you have designated as an altar? You may have a kneeler for this purpose. How does your body posture communicate to God in a way that transcends your words?

God who is worthy of all glory and praise, let me come before you, body, soul, and spirit, bringing to you my entire being as an offering that is pleasing to you, rising before you like the sweet smell of incense. Make me an "evening offering" to you so that, in me, my family, my neighbors, my co-workers, and the strangers I encounter may be given a glimpse of your great love for this world. In Christ's name. Amen.

10. PRAYING JESUS' PRAYER

"Pray like this . . ."
Matthew 6:9a

For a year during my twenties I worked as a barista at a well-known coffee shop. Before I began working, I knew little about coffee and even less about how to operate an espresso machine. But over time, others carefully trained me. I was told, "Steam the milk like this," or "Make sure the espresso shots last between 17 and 22 seconds," or "Drizzle the caramel in this pattern." Through repetition, I learned and perfected many of the skills required to make excellent coffee beverages.

Likewise, it may be the case that you know very little about prayer. But, perhaps a bit like crafting a coffee beverage, prayer is a learned skill. With encouragement and careful instruction, by God's grace we can acquire this skill.

Some of us feel inadequate or perhaps even foolish when we pray. We struggle to pray on our own, and if asked to pray before a group we are terrified! However, we can learn to pray not only from others in our church community but also from Jesus himself.

Today's Scripture is from Matthew 6. Open a Bible and find the passage. Jesus says, "Pray like this," and then he provides us with what we know as the Lord's Prayer. If you know it by heart, then you have obtained a very helpful guide for learning how to pray, not only in repeating Jesus's words but in adopting the themes present there for other concerns.

Jesus tells his disciples to petition the Father, asking that the Kingdom be present among them, thus "hallowing," or making holy, God's name. He instructs them to ask for daily provision of food and forgiveness, as well as a generous heart that extends forgiveness to others. He encourages them to ask God to watch over their paths, leading them away from pitfalls and temptations, and lastly, to trust all things to God's care.

Jesus has given you a pattern to follow. Learn from it.

Lord Jesus, teach me to pray, so that I may come before you with confidence. I am assured of your acceptance, as you have welcomed me by your tremendous grace. May I bask in that acceptance and speak my heart before you as one who is confident of being beloved. May my prayers express my deep love for you, my commitment to you, and my willingness to live for you. Amen.

TAKING A STEP

How would you describe your prayer life? There is always room for growth.

God will provide the grace needed to take a step forward.

Consider how you might make prayer a habit.

Write out your plan in a journal, on a piece of paper, or in the margin of this book.

Bible Reading

11. LEARNING TO READ

"Weren't our hearts on fire when he spoke to us along the road and when he explained the scriptures for us?"
Luke 24:32

If you are unfamiliar with the story of Jesus encountering two men on the road to Emmaus, read Luke 24:13-35. In it, the resurrected Christ appeared and spoke with these men about himself, though they did not recognize him at first.

Though we commonly refer to the companions on the road to Emmaus as disciples, they might be labeled better as "admirers."[8] It was not until Jesus opened the Scriptures to them, teaching them to read Moses and the prophets in light of Christ, that their hearts were ignited. Prior to that moment, they regarded Jesus as a failed Messiah, and because Jesus had failed, they were headed home. Before they could be transformed into disciples, the admirers had to learn to read.

Oftentimes, we are like those admirers on the road to Emmaus. We have long known about Jesus. We have heard his teachings; observed his life. But we haven't completely given ourselves over to him, for we perceive him as less than he truly is.

Once the two companions on the road to Emmaus perceived that Jesus was not a failed Messiah but the fulfillment of the very hope of Israel, they moved beyond a posture of observation and spectatorship and stepped squarely into the stream of history as followers of the one who set the world into motion. Once they saw Jesus as the one to whom the Old Testament was pointing, they understood that their allegiance could be to no one else.

The Bible assists us in becoming truly committed to Christ. Like Jesus' companions on the road to Emmaus, we must learn to read. In the Bible, we find the story of God's redemption revealed fully in the person of Jesus, and as Jesus teaches us to read this story aright, we become characters in that story. We become the actors through whom God brings about his good ends.

Jesus, I have committed my life to you. I have a desire to learn the story of the Bible in a way that helps me become a better follower. Whether I am an advanced scholar or a novice, I know that there is much to learn. There are narratives within this book that will challenge me, reshape me, and transform me. Set my heart ablaze. Amen.

12. WHO ARE YOU?

I keep your word close, in my heart,
so that I won't sin against you.
Psalm 119:9

Each day as I sit down at my desk, I am surrounded by numerous reminders of the things that matter most to me. There are pictures of my wife Molly. Nearby, in my desk drawer, is a copy of the liturgy from the day of our wedding. On my bulletin board are pieces of artwork that my daughter gave me. In addition to reminders of my family, I have other pictures, gifts, and mementos that bring memories of dear friends and of the most significant moments in my life.

These things remind me that this is who I am. Likewise, the act of opening our Bible and reading its contents grounds us, helping us remember who we are and to whom we belong. We have been created in God's image, and in Christ we have received an inheritance as a child of God. By coming to grips with our identity, we are able to act accordingly. The choices we make, whether for sin or for righteousness, are reflections of our self-understanding. Are we "lousy sinners" or "those in whom Christ dwells"?

The psalmist instructs us: By taking God's words as they are found in Scripture and placing them at the center of our being—our heart—we are able to avoid wrong behavior and sinful action. When we read our Bible daily, we internalize what we encounter. Through familiarity with the narrative accounts, the commandments, and the wisdom sayings, we are empowered to live righteous and holy lives before God.

Eugene Peterson has written, "Without this text, firmly established as the authoritative center of our communal and personal lives, we will founder. We will sink into a swamp of well-meaning but ineffectual men and women who are mired unmercifully in our needs and wants and feelings."[9] The Bible places us on solid ground.

Holy and Righteous God, the Bible is evidence of your grace. Your desire is for us to live by your way, and you have given us your word so that we might see that path and choose to follow it. May your word saturate my thoughts, so that the story of Scripture may come to permeate my life in such a way that I might live blamelessly before you, avoiding sin, and remaining pure in mind and body. In Christ's name. Amen.

13. A TRUSTWORTHY GUIDE

Every scripture is inspired by God and is useful for teaching,
for showing mistakes, for correcting, and for training character,
so that the person who belongs to God can be equipped
to do everything that is good.
2 Timothy 3:16-17

When learning a new skill, it is wise to seek and learn from those who have mastered that skill, whether it be playing an instrument, molding a piece of pottery, or perfecting a jump shot. If we open our lives to the person possessing the authority and knowledge to help us progress, then our training will naturally include correction, teaching, and steering away from common mistakes.

Just as the master of a skill, or body of knowledge, has much to offer us when consulted, so too does the Bible serve as the critical source for our formation as disciples of Jesus. All Christians, no matter how the details of their beliefs may differ, agree that the Bible is a unique source of knowledge and guidance for the individual believer and the church.

As stated in Second Timothy, the function of Scripture is clear: Scripture reveals mistakes, it corrects, and it trains. It performs these functions "so that the person who belongs to God can be equipped to do everything that is good."

A right reading of the Bible leads to a transformed life; for the Bible, read rightly, points beyond itself to the God who inspired it. Through an encounter with God as revealed in Jesus Christ, we are given the gift of the Holy Spirit, united to the Son, and adopted as sons and daughters by the Father.

The Bible is not an end in itself. It is given to us so that we might be joined to God, and transformed by God.

God, help me to learn from Scripture in the way this text describes. May I have a open heart and mind so that the Bible teaches me, uncovers my errors, corrects me when I am wrong, and refines my character. Then, let me bear fruit accordingly. Having been trained in the story of the Bible, let me live as a faithful disciple, giving witness to the truth of your word. Amen.

14. LEARNING THAT WE MIGHT SHARE

Preach the word. Be ready to do it whether it is convenient or inconvenient. Correct, confront, and encourage with patience and instruction.

2 Timothy 4:2

Jesus once told a parable wherein a farmer sows seed. Some seed falls along the path, other seed falls along the rocks, while still other seed comes to rest among soil riddled with thorns and thistles. The seed that takes root in these three places fails, for various reasons, to thrive. But there is another place where the farmer sows seed: on good soil. And it is this soil, Jesus says, that produces a yield abundantly beyond that which is expected—thirty, sixty, one hundred fold.

Jesus then explained the parable. He said the seed scattered is the word, and just as results will vary in farming, so too will the results differ when we share the word with others.

If you count yourself among those committed to Christ, you are like the farmer in the parable. You, too, are called to scatter seed, which is the word of God. This requires boldness, faithfulness, a steady confidence, and a sure commitment.

There are both explicit and subtle pressures in our world that encourage us to privatize our Christian faith. But in today's Scripture, we are told to share the word nonetheless, whether it is "convenient or inconvenient," teaching, correcting, rebuking, and patiently inviting others to consider following Jesus. Popular sentiment says, "If you have thoughts on religion, keep it to yourself." The writer of Second Timothy disagrees: "Preach the word." The command could not be more plain.

But to preach the word, one must know the word. This devotional guide provides but a sampling of Scripture. There is much more to be discovered. Take time today to read the Parable of the Soils in Mark 4, or choose another portion of Scripture to sit and soak with. Let the word permeate your mind. Internalize it. Let it shape you. And then share it. Spread some seed. Then wait to see what comes up.

Holy Spirit, to preach the word I must know the word. Imprint the knowledge I gain through reading the Bible firmly upon my heart, so that I may easily bring it to mind when presented with an opportunity to share your word with others. Let my preaching of the word always build up, encourage, steer others right, and point to you. Amen.

15. IDENTITY IN CHRIST

The word of Christ must live in you richly.
Colossians 3:16a

I am from Texas. Depending on one's perspective, this is either a virtue or an unfortunate accident of birth. Texans have a unique identity and self-understanding. They are proud of their speech, their heroes (Stephen F. Austin, Sam Houston, Davy Crockett), their legends ("Remember the Alamo!"), the days of "The Republic," their distinctive Tex-Mex cuisine, and their rich culture.

What it means to be a Texan has been imprinted upon my life. From a very early age, I was formed in the stories, culture, and practices of Texas. Upon meeting me, you can figure out pretty quickly where I'm from.

Of course, there is an aspect of my identity that is far more important than my being a Texan. I am a disciple of Jesus Christ.

My identity as a disciple of Jesus, like my identity as a Texan, is dependent upon stories, culture, and practices. The stories are given in Scripture. Therefore, the Bible must be read, studied, and discussed. And the best place for the text to be read, experienced, and understood is within the culture and practices of the church, the people of God.

As you make Bible reading a daily practice, you will obtain a deeper understanding of the story of Israel and the words and work of Jesus. In this way, according to today's Scripture, the "word of Christ" will come to "live in you richly." You will more fully grasp the hope of Israel and will see how Christ himself is the realization of that hope. If you read prayerfully, by the assistance of the Holy Spirit your reading of the Bible should result in a deepening love for God and neighbor.

As the Bible shapes your identity in Christ, Jesus points you to others—to serve, to share, and to witness.

Lord, it is my desire that your word would take root in me as a living, active force. I want to think, speak, and act as a new creature, transformed by your power. As I read the Bible, I pray that I would become not as the scribes and Pharisees, who knew their Scriptures well but did not derive life from their study. Instead, let me be so richly alive, so renewed, so radically different, that your reality would be undeniably manifest. Let the Bible lead me to Christ. Then, let Christ in me lead others to you. Amen.

16. PUTTING IT INTO PRACTICE

You must be doers of the word and not only
hearers who mislead themselves.
James 1:22

Over the past several years I have worked as a school bus driver. Bus drivers must execute runs safely, deliver passengers on time, and foster a healthy environment that supplements students' educational experience during the day. We provide an important service in the lives of communities, transporting people on field trips, to athletic contests, and to and from home.

Bus drivers have endless reminders of one important aspect of our job each and every day: no child should be left unattended on the bus, ever. To this end, our dispatcher exhorts us over the radio. We have signs reminding us that state, "I care, I search." We have an electronic device at the rear of each bus designed to monitor whether the driver walks to the back, making sure the bus is empty, at the conclusion of the route.

Despite all these reminders, occasionally children are left behind on the bus. Drivers do fail. They may have heard the messages to search, to be diligent, to be careful, but for various reasons they do not do what they have been told.

The Bible is likewise filled with messages and reminders that guide us in wisdom and faithfulness. We are not only to read them or hear them; we are to do them. We are charged to "love the Lord with heart, mind, soul, and strength," "to love our neighbor as ourselves," and many other vital commands.

But as James says, we must not only hear the word, but do it. Tend to the message of the Bible. Pay attention to the countless reminders of what Scripture commands, and put what you find into practice.

God Almighty, you spoke by prophets and priests and faithful servants long ago. After my life comes to its end, your word will remain; so while I live, let your word dwell in me. Let me hear it, and when I hear it, let me do it. Let me live obediently according to what you have spoken. Your word is eternal and sure. I can stake my life on it. Ignite my passion for your truth as it is contained in the Bible. May it burn bright all of my days. Amen.

TAKING A STEP

How often do you read the Bible?

Decide today to make this a regular practice.

Find a Bible reading plan, or choose a book to study carefully in the weeks and months ahead.

Be intentional.

Worship

17. A RESPONSE
OF WONDER

*Greatness and grandeur are in front of him; strength and joy
are in his place. Give to the Lord, all families of the nations—give
to the Lord glory and power! Give to the Lord the glory
due his name! Bring gifts! Enter his presence!
Bow down to the Lord in holy splendor!*
1 Chronicles 16:27-29

One Christmas morning when I was a child, I entered our
family living room with my sister, overwhelmed by the quantity
of gifts. After opening each one, I turned to my father and
exclaimed, "It's just what I've always been wanting!"

The gifts given to me evoked a response of wonder. I did
not have to manufacture my response, for my excitement was
a natural outflow of the magnitude of the event. My reaction
was proportionate to my amazement at the gifts.

Worship should evoke a similar response. Worship is not so much a matter of willpower as it is the realization of wonder. If you struggle in your desire to worship, it may be because you have yet to grasp God's love as revealed in Jesus Christ.

According to today's Scripture, the glory we ascribe to God is not something that we conjure in our imagination; it is something that is deserved. It is God's "due." What might this mean?

The church proclaims Christ through the gospel—the announcement of forgiveness through his death on the cross. This forgiveness is available to anyone by faith, regardless of age, race, economic status, or any other classification that divides us. But this "due" is something we can never fully repay, for the magnitude of the gift is infinite in scope. Therefore, our wonderment expressed in worship should never cease, for the gospel will always contain some hidden dimension that we can newly ponder and appreciate.

Christ is the rightful object of your desires. He is "just what you've always been wanting." Look upon him. Let him stir your soul.

Holy and Blessed Father, you are worthy of all glory and praise. You have done mighty and wondrous works, culminating in the incarnation, death, and resurrection of your Son, Jesus Christ. Let me look upon him and discover the motivation for worship. Let me have a glimpse of the magnitude of his love for me—yes even for me!—the one who willingly laid down his life for the sin of the world. Amen.

18. SING ANYWAY

I will praise God's name with song;
I will magnify him with thanks.
Psalm 69:30

When I was a high school student, I was reluctant to sing hymns. In retrospect, I am thankful for a friend who encouraged me to sing anyway, though I did not heed that advice until later.

Singing in worship has the power to open our souls to the transforming power of God's grace. When you do not feel like singing, sing anyway. The effect may surprise you.

C. S. Lewis, upon returning to Christianity after a foray as an atheist, found the hymnody unappealing. He remarked, "I disliked very much their hymns, which I considered to be fifth-rate poems set to sixth-rate music." He would be much better off reading theology and thinking deeply concerning the things of God, he thought, than he could ever be gathering with his Anglican congregation and singing songs set to melodies he found distasteful.

After some time, however, Lewis observed, "But as I went on I saw the merit of it. I came up against different people of quite different outlooks and different education, and then gradually my conceit just began peeling off. I realized that the hymns, which were just sixth-rate music, were, nevertheless, being sung with devotion and benefit by an old saint in elastic-side boots in the opposite pew, then you realize that you aren't fit to clean those boots. It gets you out of your solitary conceit."[10]

In worship, we sing hymns and praise songs to express our faithfulness and devotion to God. In many faith traditions, the songs chosen for worship are as significant as the sermons preached and the prayers prayed.

Through singing, proper doctrine is imparted to the hearers, and truth moved from the head to the heart. Christian truth should not only enable right thinking but also right feeling. Combined, right thinking and right feeling yield right living, or a transformed life. For those committed to Christ, all dimensions of the human person are changed through discipleship, and one avenue for discipleship runs through the singing of songs.

Praise God's name with song. Magnify him with thanks. And rejoice as God transforms your heart in accordance with Christ-likeness.

Lord, may I sing your praises all day long. May I bless you with my lips, and joyously give thanks. In Christ's name. Amen.

19. COMING TOGETHER TO BECOME HOLY

Let's also think about how to motivate each other to show love and to do good works. Don't stop meeting together with other believers, which some people have gotten into the habit of doing. Instead, encourage each other, especially as you see the day drawing near.
Hebrews 10:24-25

After many years in youth ministry, as volunteer and as pastor, there is one thing of which I am sure: growth in holiness is dependent upon the health and cohesion of the community. This applies to congregations as a whole, as well as to any other form of discipleship.

You may be tempted to live your life as a solitary Christian. You may believe church gatherings are empty forms of religion and of little spiritual benefit. This stream of thought is as old as human history, though perhaps more prevalent today. The recipients of the epistle to the Hebrews had to be reminded, "Don't stop meeting together with other believers, which some people have gotten into the habit of doing." Those words could just as well be addressed to us today.

Christians gather together each week to do more than sing songs, offer prayers, and ingest a sermon. They come together to become holy and to imagine new ways of demonstrating to others God's work of redemption, which has been accomplished in Jesus Christ. We are to "think about how to motivate each other to show love and to do good works." We do not gather simply so that we, as individuals, obtain benefit. We gather so that we might bless both one another and the city, township, or village within which God has placed us.

Community should serve the purposes cited by the writer of Hebrews: we motivate each other to show love and do good works. When this happens, we exhibit health, and when the worshiping community is engaging Jesus in this way, doing what he commands, holiness follows.

God Almighty, the gathering of your saints together in worship is not an end in itself, but is intended to become a space wherein we spur one another on to show love and to do good works. Fix this in my mind and seal it upon my heart, and enable me, alongside other Christians, to live this vision of community, so that we might be a blessing to all people. In Jesus's name, Amen.

20. WHAT KIND OF TREE ARE YOU?

"You will know them by their fruit. Do people get bunches of
grapes from thorny weeds, or do they get figs from thistles?
In the same way, every good tree produces good fruit,
and every rotten tree produces bad fruit. A good tree can't produce
bad fruit. And a rotten tree can't produce good fruit. Every tree that
doesn't produce good fruit is chopped down and thrown
into the fire. Therefore, you will know them by their fruit."
Matthew 7:16-20

What kind of person are you? What is your life producing?
Are you a person who naturally and easily does the things that
God commands you to do in Scripture? Are you a person who
displays "love, joy, peace, patience, kindness, goodness, gentleness, and self-control?" Do you want to be? Do you believe this
is the kind of life Jesus offers?

Even Christians find this hard to believe. But it is true. Christ
offers a renewed character, as referred to in today's Scripture.
This illustration in Matthew 7 may be my favorite saying of
Jesus, for the imagery is so vivid.

Jesus makes an observation: Good trees produce good fruit,
and bad trees produce bad fruit. By making this observation, he

is posing a question: what kind of tree are you? Character, Jesus is saying, determines how we speak and act. We produce fruit in accordance with our character.

Though it may be hard for us to admit, even our righteousness can be born of wrong motivation. Jesus accused the Pharisees of being "whitewashed tombs," performing all the right actions but inside being full of rottenness and death. It is counterintuitive but true that we are called to repent of not only our sin but our righteousness, relying instead fully on Christ's righteousness.

The worshiping community, the church, is the space we enter to be trained as disciples of Jesus. Worship, rightly focused upon God, renders us new creatures. Our hearts are transformed. We are made holy. And our lives then begin to evidence this transformation before the world. Worship is not behavior modification but renovation, all to God's glory.

Holy Spirit, help me to love the church. Help me to see the body of Christ as the crucible wherein my character might be formed anew in Christ, the place where I can be made like a good tree that produces good fruit, all to your glory. Amen.

21. In Spirit and in Truth

"But the time is coming—and is here!—when true worshippers will worship in spirit and in truth. God is spirit, and it is necessary to worship God in spirit and in truth."
John 4:23-24

During graduate school, one of my colleagues told me of her experience growing up in the Pentecostal tradition. She spoke of the joy and ecstasy in worship, but lamented her experience of encountering anti-intellectualism in the preaching and a number of the group studies. I told her of my experience growing up in the Baptist tradition, where I discovered a deep passion for knowledge, yet I did not find my heart always engaged. For both of us, something had been missing.

In John 4, Jesus encounters an astute theologian—a Samaritan woman, whom he meets at Jacob's well. Their conversation touches on a wide range of topics, among these the difference between the worship of the Jews and the Samaritans. Though these two groups shared similarities in heritage, they differed in practice and in their claims of proper belief. Jesus reveals himself to her as the Messiah of Israel and announces that, through him, worship of God has undergone both a renewal and a transformation. True worship, says Jesus, encompasses both spirit and truth.

Jesus is not only concerned with the fervor and passion of our worship; he is also concerned with the subject of worship. Jesus instructs us that "it is necessary to worship God in spirit and in truth," a puzzling phrase that grabs our attention. What does this mean? Jesus calls us to know God as God, thus worshiping truthfully. We are also to experience God as God truly is, resting our spirit upon our heart's true home—the One who formed us in our mother's womb, who knows us inside and out.

Jesus's call to worship God in "spirit and in truth" encompasses both our mental and our emotional faculties. True worship engages the whole person, enabling us to increase in our knowledge of God and our love for God. We are then sent into the world to serve God with our hands, putting what we have received on display, pointing others back to Christ.

God, help me to know you as you truly are, and to experience you in the fullness of joy. Renew both my mind and my heart, so that I might worship you in spirit and in truth. Amen.

22. Offering Ourselves

So, brothers and sisters, because of God's mercies, I encourage you to present your bodies as a living sacrifice that is holy and pleasing to God. This is your appropriate priestly service.
Romans 12:1

The word worship brings to the imagination an event, most notably a standard church service. But the biblical notion of worship moves us beyond an event and thrusts us forward to a constant way of life. The worship of God is not only marked by the words we say and hear but is defined by action.

One of the sayings of the Desert Fathers, a group of fourth and fifth century Egyptian monks, reflects this sentiment well: "Abba James said: We do not want words alone, for there are too many words among people today. What we need is action, for that is what we are looking for, not words which do not bear fruit."[11]

True worship of God, that which engages God at the level of mind, body, and spirit, results in a new way of engaging with the world. The love of God should yield the love of neighbor.

Our worship of God should transcend what we do when we gather with other saints for the celebration of liturgy, the singing of hymns, the hearing of a sermon, and the praying of prayers.

Worship of God should permeate every action undertaken in both our ordinary and extraordinary moments. Our bodies should be a "living sacrifice," offered continually in service to God's purposes for our world.

This type of action includes serving the poor. It includes placing the welfare of others before our own concerns. It includes advocacy for the oppressed, the widow, and the orphan. It may even include putting ourselves at risk so that others might prosper and live.

These ideas should resonate with those committed to Christ, for Jesus did nothing less. The imitation of Christ is an evidence of our worship and our discipleship. We do these things because we worship a God who likewise did these things on our behalf; and all the while we fall at his feet as we come to a deep realization of the abundance he has provided through his death and resurrection.

Loving and Merciful God, help me to turn my entire life over to you, so that my actions might bring you joy. Help me to remember that my body should be offered to you as a "living sacrifice." In Christ's name. Amen.

TAKING A STEP

Do you regularly engage in worship?

Worship connects us with God and with other Christians so that we might be built up and equipped to better carry out God's mission in our world.

Resolve today to worship God in formal gatherings, and through the way that you live.

Witness

23. TELLING OTHERS ABOUT JESUS

"Rather, you will receive power when the Holy Spirit has come upon you, and you will be my witnesses in Jerusalem, in all Judea and Samaria, and to the end of the earth."
Acts 1:8

This verse of Scripture will forever be imprinted on my brain. Why? A teacher insisted, and gave me a homework assignment that left me no choice.

My teacher demanded that I learn the lesson of observation well. So, with Acts 1:8 as my focus, I was asked to derive twenty-five observations. Terms, sentence structure, parts of speech, and context were all fair game. I struggled to complete the task.

Upon turning in my twenty-five observations, I felt I knew the text well. Then my teacher gave me another assignment: twenty-five more observations.

Though these exercises were meant to teach a Bible study method, what was accomplished transcended that single aim. Through pondering this text, I came to understand the meaning of witness, and to realize that the task of witness begins locally but is meant to extend to all the created order.

The book of Acts makes clear that by the power of the Holy Spirit, followers of Jesus are to point to his person and his deeds. We are to witness to who God is and what God has done. And by witnessing to God's person and God's accomplishments, we are to announce the gospel of Jesus Christ. By virtue of God's character revealed in Christ and his atoning death on the cross, all people can be reconciled to God and to one another.

Like the first disciples in the book of Acts, we are to witness. We must point others to Christ. And we are given power to accomplish this task by virtue of the Holy Spirit. We are not alone in the work; therefore, fear not. As you tell others about Jesus, be confident that the Holy Spirit is with you, helping you to speak and to act in a way that directs others to Christ.

Holy Spirit, I trust that you are with me in the task of witness. Help me point others to Jesus Christ, who has made salvation possible for those who put their faith in him. I want others to see you and come to know you. Use my life to draw others to you. Amen.

24. GIVEN THE OPPORTUNITY

Act wisely toward outsiders, making the most of the opportunity. Your
speech should always be gracious and sprinkled with insight so that
you may know how to respond to every person.
Colossians 4:5-6

On my school bus one afternoon, two sixth-grade students carefully attempted to define atheist and atheism. An older student spoke up. "I'm an atheist," he said. The students then listened to what this student believed. I also listened with interest. I like to call such moments "research."

Soon thereafter, one of the students, who is a Christian, spoke up: "Ben, aren't you a pastor?" I laughed and said, "Of sorts." The topic of religion was not broached for the remainder of the ride, but a declaration had been made, both on the existence of God and the non-existence of God.

As I reflected on that exchange, I couldn't help put that moment into the context of an ongoing relationship. Each day, I interact with my students, including this young atheist. I do my very best to treat each student with respect and dignity. I try and listen carefully to concerns and to be fair in handing out punishment when students cause trouble. I do this not only because it is right, or because I wish to be a good employee. I do this because I am a representative, a witness, of Jesus Christ. My service is given on behalf of another, the Lord of all.

Each day, we are presented with countless opportunities to witness to Jesus. Our text from Colossians instructs us: our words "should always be gracious and sprinkled with insight." The form of our witness can take many forms. We may be given the opportunity to tell someone the story of Christ. We might have the chance to share wisdom from Scripture or from a church service or Sunday school class. We might simply share some bit of knowledge we have gained along life's way in a kind and helpful manner.

Every interaction we have is an opportunity to provide a glimpse of God's grace. Be a witness.

Glorious and Blessed God, give me wisdom. Help me to know how to speak to those within and outside the family of faith. Help me to display your wisdom and love through gracious speech and insightful words. By your grace, may I lead others to you. In Christ's name. Amen.

25. A THOUGHTFUL RESPONSE

Whenever anyone asks you to speak of your hope,
be ready to defend it.
1 Peter 3:15b

I have yet to encounter a Christian who does not wish to share their faith with others. But not everyone feels comfortable and confident with the calling to share Christ with others. Friends and fellow Christians have spoken to me concerning the words to say, or have struggled to derive a way of inviting others to follow Jesus that is natural and respectful.

There are two separate tasks involved in witnessing to Christ. The first is evangelism, and the second is apologetics. Evangelism is the act of sharing the gospel. Apologetics is a theological discipline that seeks to both defend and commend the Christian faith.

Alister McGrath writes this concerning the difference between evangelism and apologetics: "A rough working definition of evangelism might be 'inviting someone to become a Christian.' Apologetics could then be thought of as clearing the ground for that invitation so that it is more likely to receive a positive response."

Witnessing to Jesus is a two-fold task. It includes inviting others to the life of discipleship and answering the doubts, questions, and difficulties of those inside and outside the church concerning Christianity. Offering a helpful analogy, McGrath continues, "Evangelism could be said to be like offering someone bread. Apologetics would then be about persuading people there is bread to be had and it is good to eat."[12]

When we are asked concerning our hope, First Peter instructs us to "be ready to defend it." We are actively to seek answers that address the questions our world is asking, and to respond in thoughtful, reasonable ways.

You may feel ill equipped to witness to others. But let me encourage you: If you desire to grow in knowledge of the Christian faith, there are resources to help you, foremost among them the presence of the Holy Spirit. Ask God to guide you to the presence of others who can train you to articulate what Christians believe and why, so that when you are asked about your hope in Christ, you can provide an answer that gives him glory and honor.

Lord Jesus, my hope rests in you. Equip me to answer questions in a reasonable and intelligent manner, so that your truth may be known and experienced. In your holy name. Amen.

26. ON AN ADVENTURE

Jesus sent these twelve out and commanded them . . .
"As you go, make this announcement: 'The Kingdom of
heaven has come near.' Heal the sick, raise the dead,
cleanse those with skin diseases, and throw out demons."
Matthew 10:5-8a

Stanley Hauerwas and William Willimon memorably expressed the calling of Jesus in the New Testament this way: "The Gospels make wonderfully clear that the disciples had not the foggiest idea of what they had gotten into when they followed Jesus. With a simple, 'Follow me,' Jesus invited ordinary people to come out and be part of an adventure, a journey that kept surprising them at every turn in the road."[13]

Not much has changed. The disciples were incredibly like us, and we are incredibly like the disciples. We have "not the foggiest idea" of what Jesus has called us to. Announce the kingdom? Heal the sick? Cleanse lepers? Cast out demons? Raise the dead?

"Who, me?"

Yes, you.

We too have been called on the adventure. We have been caught up in God's salvific work. We are not spectators, but participants. The task of the witness is to give testimony to that which we have seen and heard. God has been at work, and you are invited to take part.

Our reading provides us with excellent instruction for the two-fold nature of witness. Jesus's command encompasses physical and spiritual needs. Jesus does not just say, "Announce the Kingdom"; nor does he only say, "Heal the sick." Witnessing to the Kingdom in a faithful manner includes calling people to conversion and new birth, as well as feeding the hungry, clothing the naked, and protecting the needy.

There is not a single dimension of human existence that the gospel of Jesus Christ leaves untouched. If you have been caught up in the story of Scripture, God through you can heal the sick, raise the dead, cleanse the leper, cast out demons, and give evidence of God's reign. You have been invited to take part in a grand adventure.

God Almighty, if I have ever thought your calling on my life was boring, I repent! You have made me a part of your adventure and invited me to announce the coming of another world. Help me to be a faithful witness. May your reign take hold in my life, so that I might give evidence to your Kingdom. Amen.

27. SHARING WHAT
WE HAVE LEARNED

So, my child, draw your strength from the grace that
is in Christ Jesus. Take the things you heard me say in
front of many other witnesses and pass them on to
faithful people who are also capable of teaching others.
2 Timothy 2:1-2

My first two years as a school bus driver, I was not assigned a regular route. Instead, I filled in for other drivers who were unable to complete their duties that day, or I rode along with others when my services were not needed. Each ride provided me with an opportunity to learn.

When I was on my own, I learned from the students. But when I was with another driver, I asked questions. I learned as much as I could from other drivers so that I could perform my responsibilities more effectively. Though this type of instruction was informal, I gained just as much, if not more, in these conversations than I had during preliminary job-training sessions.

Since that time, other drivers have riden along with me who are new to the company, and I have done my best to impart knowledge when I have been asked to share what I now know.

Disciples of Jesus are called to a similar task. We are to take those things we learned from faithful pastors and teachers and pass them along to others. We are to witness to Christ and the trustworthiness of his way of life and to instruct others how they, too, can follow as his disciples.

It may be that the primary setting for witnessing may be at home. You may have a spouse who does not believe. If your children are young, you are called to instruct them patiently in the ways of the Lord. If your children are old, do not despair, but love them as Christ loved you. Pray for them. Serve them. Speak to them of your hope when you have the opportunity.

Others may have the gift of evangelism and are naturally inclined to steer conversations with new friends and old acquaintances toward faith. Whether to our close connections or loose ties, we are called to witness.

Father in Heaven, assist me in taking what I have received and passing it on to others. Give me the skills to witness faithfully to Christ through word and deed. Amen.

28. PASSING THE INVITATION ON

"Therefore, go and make disciples of all nations, baptizing them in the name of the Father and of the Son and of the Holy Spirit, teaching them to obey everything that I've commanded you. Look, I myself will be with you every day until the end of this present age."
Matthew 28:19-20

When I lived in the Dallas area, I frequently shared a pew with an elderly gentlemen who was passionate about evangelism in prisons. Each week he visited prisoners, and each week he returned to church with a card. Written on the card was a number, and the number represented those he had led to profess faith in Christ the week before. I never saw the number, but I had heard this was his practice. I was impressed by his devotion and passion. But I was not that kind of evangelist.

You may not be, either. But there is pressure among Christians to be winsome in this way. However, the words of Christ above tell us that the task of evangelism not only includes leading others to conversion but also to make "disciples," as Jesus commanded. Another word that could be used is "apprentices." These apprentices are to "obey everything" that Jesus commands. And for this task, Jesus promises his presence. The disciple-making task is not undertaken alone.

In this way, more of us than we realize may qualify as evangelists. We not only witness to Christ by pointing others to him, but by teaching his ways. We announce Jesus as Lord, inviting others to live under his reign.

William J. Abraham has written, "We can best improve our thinking on evangelism by conceiving it as that set of intentional activities which is governed by the goal of initiating people into the kingdom of God for the first time."[14] In other words, the task of evangelism should not only be concerned with telling people about Jesus but also equipping them to live as citizens of God's kingdom. Faithful witness includes not only an invitation to believe, but to follow.

Lord Jesus, I have heard your call to make disciples of all nations. Help me to invite others to follow after you, to trust you, and to learn from you. I have committed my life to you. Make me like you, so that through me others might come to know what you are like. Amen.

TAKING A STEP

When was the last time you had a conversation with another person about your faith?

Jesus Christ calls us to follow him, and along the way we are charged with the task of inviting others to take part in what God is doing.

Look for opportunities to share your faith.

Pray that God will give you courage.

Trust that the Holy Spirit will help you as you earnestly seek to witness to Christ.

Financial Giving

29. MINE OR YOURS?

The earth is the Lord's, and everything in it,
the world and its inhabitants too.
Psalm 24:1

As a parent of a two-year-old, I frequently hear the word *mine*. My daughter, who claims ownership, holds tight to phones, cameras, and other expensive pieces of technology. When my wife Molly and I need to use these items, she emphatically tells us that they are not ours. Needless to say, these exchanges give us the opportunity to teach our little one a host of important values.

Foremost among these lessons is that in some sense, everything we receive is a gift, a possession that we steward only for a time. This is even the case for those things we come to think of as uniquely ours. It is a lesson that is easily forgotten, even if it is learned well in childhood.

The Bible begins with God's creation of the world. In Genesis 1, God turns the stewardship of creation over to human beings, who as male and female are created in God's image. They are to care for and steward the creation, working diligently to bring about its flourishing. And they are to do so as God's representatives, for the earth remains God's possession, the fruit of his labors. The psalmist reminds us of this: "The earth is the Lord's, and everything in it."

This truth has tremendous implications for our understanding of financial giving. All our possessions are gifts that have been given to us and that we are to steward and put to good use. The portion we return to God through the tithe or other special gifts is a recognition of the origin of all that we possess. God has graciously provided us with all we have, whether through financial prosperity or the health, mental acumen, and diligence that was necessary for us to obtain what we have earned.

Financial giving is a much more inviting proposition when we first declare to God, "It's all yours!"

Generous God, help me to see all that I have as yours, whether I have much or little. As Paul wrote to the church at Philippi, help me to be "content in all things." With the gifts I have received from you, help me use them in a way that accomplishes your purposes in the world. Help me to be generous with my finances. Help me to give to those that are in need. Amen.

30. Giving in Response

*You must reserve a tenth-part of whatever
your fields produce each year.*
Deuteronomy 14:22

I grew up as part of a church community. In that community, there was never a time that finances were discussed in any way other than with a straightforward expectation that for church members, a tithe was simply part of a disciple's life. The word "tithe" means "tenth-part" and has been understood as returning to God one-tenth of everything one yields through work. Tithing, as an important Christian practice, was discussed within my church as a sign of spiritual health and a generous heart. Therefore, when I began to earn my own money, calculating a "tenth-part" and placing it in the offering plate was quite natural.

This is not the case for every person who grew up in church. There are those who hear exhortations to tithe as greedy appeals, or teachings to give financially as subtle and not-so-subtle messages that impart guilt. Churches have responded by talking less about our finances, or by softening their rhetoric so as not to offend anyone.

But the Bible is unapologetic in discussing our income, possessions, and generous giving. In the Old Testament, the offering was not determined by a percentage of income, but instead consisted of sacrificing a portion of crop and livestock yields. The act of sacrifice had a number of purposes, among them atoning for sin and caring for the poor and oppressed. In the New Testament, the practice of giving continued, described most powerfully in Second Corinthians 8 and 9.

For Christians, financial giving is not an act of righteousness to earn God's favor. Nor is it an atonement for sins, as though turning over a portion of our money would justify our standing before God. Christ has already done these things! Instead, financial giving is a response of worship. God has generously given us the gift of life in the Son as preeminent among all other gifts. In light of this, we are asked in turn to use our many lesser gifts, including our income, to bless others in the way we have been generously blessed through God's grace.

Lord, help me to give of my income proportionately, using the "tenth-part" as a baseline standard. If it be your will, help me to grow beyond that mark in generosity and love, using my financial resources to bless others. Amen.

31. To Be Bold in Generosity

Bring the whole tenth-part to the storage house so there might be food in my house. Please test me in this, says the Lord of heavenly forces. See whether I do not open all the windows of heavens for you and empty out a blessing until there is enough.

Malachi 3:10

Tithing does bring with it a blessing. Properly considered, this text teaches us of God's provision and God's abundance, both readily at hand.

In the book of Malachi, the people of Israel were challenged to return to the faithful practice of the tithe. After they returned from exile, the normalization of civic life was the priority. The observance of sacrifice and obedience to the covenant was yet to thrive. Warnings to flee false gods and return to Yahweh are key themes within this short, prophetic book.

Like the people of Israel, we are called to make sacrifices to God. We are called to give of our time, talent, and treasure in the service of God. Yet often we do not. We are deceived in thinking either that there is not enough, or that God will not provide. So we hold back. We live with a scarcity mentality, like the people of Israel, who did not bring sacrifices for fear of lack.

But our Scripture today tells us we need not fear. The challenge is given: "Test me in this." God has provided you with not only enough but an abundance. God has provided for you in the past, and will continue to provide. Think of the good that God can do with your gifts, extended with an open hand. You will see that with the giving of the gift comes a blessing—not necessarily a financial return, but joy. Joy in the deep realization that the gifts you have given were first provided for you by God's grace, and the gifts you release came from an abundance of what you already indeed possessed.

Jesus, in you we find all that we need for the journey of life, and the ability to reassess all that we have in light of your abundance. You have not only provided us with enough, but more than enough. May we in turn learn from you how to open our hands and to give freely, trusting that you will continue to give us an abundance as we progress in our discipleship to you. In your name. Amen.

32. GIFTS THAT MATTER

Jesus called his disciples to him and said, "I assure you that this poor widow has put in more than everyone who's been putting money in the treasury."
Mark 12:43

When I was a high school student, my church was in need of a new building. A plan was made, the cost was counted, and the vision was proclaimed to the people. A number of avenues were given by which people could contribute. Some church members donated classic cars or property. An elderly couple gave their wedding rings, which the church later returned. But I was most impressed by something smaller.

I was most impressed by the gifts of the children. Our children's ministry provided containers for collecting change. As these containers were returned, a tally was taken and the amount was announced to the church. Though I do not remember the total, I do remember being humbled and inspired.

There is an unfortunate myth that prevails among the rank and file of Christian people that the only gifts that can truly make a difference are those that are large, extravagant, and impressive. It is not so. In our reading today, we learn from Jesus that it is not the amount that counts most before God, but the motivation. For gifts large and small, it is the heart that matters most.

The children in my church gave without pretense and without an expectation of return. They did not expect others to esteem them more highly, or for people to speak well of them. They gave because they were asked and because it was right.

So too did the widow. She gave two small coins. The gift was meager, but Jesus was impressed. He knew and understood the sacrifice. He also knew that she gave with the right motivation, unlike so many others. She humbly wished to serve God in her poverty, so that in the giving of the gift she might become rich. We have much to learn from her example.

God, let me carry today the story of the widow who gave pennies to your treasury, and yet Jesus said that she had given an amount exceeding all other gifts. Help me to remember both her generosity and her heart, and so be transformed into a person who is able to give without reservation and with purity of intention. Amen.

33. ULTIMATE THINGS

"Instead, collect treasures for yourselves in heaven, where moth and rust don't eat them and where thieves don't break in and steal them. Where your treasure is, there your heart will be also."
Matthew 6:20-21

Popular investment firms entice us through advertising to allocate our money wisely so that we can enjoy retirement, prosper financially, and experience security. Yet markets ebb and flow, and those who invest their money could lose a great deal in a lagging economy, a prolonged recession, or a worldwide collapse.

Jesus tells us we should "collect treasures in heaven." We should put our resources toward the eternal. Our finances, service, and speech should be measured in light of the fullness of God's coming Kingdom. Though we should be wise in how we steward our finances today, our ultimate hope is in God.

If you put stock in bumper sticker wisdom, it is true that "He who dies with the most toys, still dies." But the hope of Christians is that this life is not all there is and that, though our mortal bodies will one day expire, we look forward to a day wherein we will be raised with Christ, clothed in immortality.

At one time, I thought that financial giving was simply a matter of determined obedience. Though I still believe that we must declare our intention to give and be generous, I have since realized that the ease of our giving is proportionate to our grasp of what we have received.

Invest in the eternal. Be a good steward of your life, and take the material resources that God gives you to use in service of the Kingdom. As it is written in Colossians 3, "Set your heart on things above." When you do so, financial generosity will be a natural outcome, for we worship a God who is generous. If you struggle with the discipline of giving, think deeply concerning how much God in Christ has given for you. God's action in Christ will melt your heart.

Holy Lord, I know that the things of this world are passing away, though it is hard to recall this truth moment by moment. Let me remember the words of Jesus, who powerfully reminds me to invest in that which is eternal, and to set my heart on you, the One who will never pass away. Amen.

34. DISCOVERING
GREATER JOY

Everyone should give whatever they have decided in their heart.
They shouldn't give with hesitation or because of pressure.
God loves a cheerful giver.
2 Corinthians 9:7

Dallas Willard once observed, "The acid test for any theology is this: Is the God presented one that can be loved heart, soul, mind, and strength?"[15]

How beautiful is your conception of God? How deeply have you come to know and appreciate the love of Christ? If you have yet to see God as the most magnificent, benevolent, and gracious being in the cosmos, keep looking. The more fully you come to grasp God as revealed in Christ, the more you will grow in your desire to give. You will find "whatever [you] have decided to give in your heart" begin to change. You will discover greater joy in giving, for you will know the One to whom you give. And your discipline of financial giving will not be regarded as an act of begrudging obedience, but an act of deep joy and worship. You will grow to be a generous person, for we worship a generous God.

This kind of transformation, if it takes hold in your life and in your church, will have manifold results. What would be said of your church in your town if your generosity became widely known? What if your church really was comprised of "cheerful givers," those who gave freely and with concern for the poor? What if your church gladly served the needs of many, and constantly sought to bless others without any expectation of return?

What would this say about our God? Your motivation for giving should not be your own acclaim, but the celebration of the God of Abraham, Isaac, and Jacob. It is the name of God that should be renowned.

Giving is therefore not simply a matter of obedience, but a matter of witness. It is an act of love for both God and neighbor. It is an evidence of manifold grace.

Gracious Father, you are the giver of every good and perfect gift. May I rejoice in you! May my love for you result in a love for generosity, for you are generous and good. May my gifts be given with joy as a blessing to you and to my neighbor who is in need, and may my giving be an extension of my true heart's desire. Amen.

TAKING A STEP

Do you offer a portion of your finances to God's work in the world?

Carefully evaluate your practice of financial giving, and commit to growth in this area, however small.

If you already make this a practice, pray and ask God if you can be even more generous.

Thoughtfully discern how best to steward your finances.

Service

35. A WAY OF LIFE

" 'I assure you that when you have done it for one of the least of
these brothers and sisters of mine, you have done it for me.' "
Matthew 25:40b

The parable Jesus tells in Matthew 25:31-46 is familiar. If
you do not know it, please take a few minutes to read it. He
describes the coming of the king, sitting on the throne of judgment. Before him are many people, whom he divides to his left
and his right, as the sheep and the goats.

To those on his right, he says they have done well, for they
fed him when he was hungry, clothed him when he was naked,
offered drink to him when he was thirsty, comforted him when
he was sick, welcomed him when he was a stranger, and visited
him when he was in prison. Perplexed, they ask, "When have we
done these things for you?" The king replies, "When you have
done it for one of the least of these . . . you have done it for me."

The exchange with those on the king's left follows the same pattern, with the key difference being that they failed to do these very same things. Those on the right receive a reward. Those on the left are sent away to punishment. The king's verdict may not be uplifting, but that is the way the story reads. When we serve "the least of these," the stakes are high.

For followers of Jesus, feeding the hungry, providing drink to the thirsty, comforting the sick, visiting the prisoner, and welcoming the stranger are not optional. These actions are the natural outflow of a life of discipleship to Christ.

Get your hands dirty. Serve in a soup kitchen, a clothing closet, or a justice ministry. Make it your way of life. Do it as an act of discipleship to Jesus. Invite him along to teach you, and expect him to be there, preparing the way, before you ever arrive. God will use these acts of obedience to change your heart, to transform you through abounding grace.

Lord, you have called me to serve the hungry, the thirsty, the sick, the prisoner, and the stranger. When I meet these persons, may I see you, and may I serve them as though I am serving you. Each and every day, may I see Christ in the people that I meet, and may I love them as such, humbly meeting every need. Amen.

36. Happy in Hope

Don't hesitate to be enthusiastic—be on fire in the Spirit as you serve the Lord! Be happy in your hope, stand your ground when you're in trouble, and devote yourselves to prayer.

Romans 12:11-12

N. T. Wright asserted, "Once we see who Jesus is, we are not only summoned to follow him in worship, love, and adoration, but to shape our world by reflecting his glory into it."[16] We are called to give Christ not only our allegiance but also our service in the world.

Our passage today names three marks of Spirit-filled, enthusiastic service: happy in hope, steadfast in trouble, and devoted to prayer. In Christ, you have nothing to fear, for God has accomplished all things necessary for redemption. In Christ, you have nothing to fear, for God is with you even when you are persecuted or in danger. In Christ, you have nothing to fear, for God is no more than a breath away, ready to hear your every plea and petition.

The New Testament gospel accounts portray Jesus as one full of enthusiasm, filled with the Spirit of God, and driven by his Father's will. Those committed to Christ will conduct themselves this way as well. Jesus had the Kingdom to announce, the people to teach, the sick to be healed, the dead to raise, the outcasts to restore, the captives to free, and the poor to dignify. There was no shortage of work.

It is the same today. Jesus calls us to follow his example and to do that which he taught. Think of your community. If that is too broad, think of your church. What are the needs? Still too vague? Think of your home. As Mother Teresa has written, "Bring love into your own home for this is where our love for others must start."[17]

Start small, in the immediacy of your life as it is today. Be filled with the Spirit. Be enthusiastic. And evidence great love.

Lord, help me to be happy in hope, steadfast in trouble, and devoted to prayer. Let me evidence enthusiasm in service, for there is work to do. Let me serve first those who are closest to me, doing so in love. Call me forth from there to feed the hungry, heal the sick, and raise the dead in both the church and the world. The needs are great. Let me respond to your call. In Christ's name. Amen.

37. Doing What Jesus Does

"So which one is greater, the one who is seated at the table or the one who serves at the table? Isn't it the one who is seated at the table? But I am among you as one who serves."

Luke 22:27

While Jesus gathered with his disciples for the Passover meal, an argument arose concerning who was the greatest. Jesus had entered the city of Jerusalem, and the twelve could sense that in him a new day had dawned. They would lead a revolution, overtaking the old powers of Rome and the corrupt priesthood. They would set things right by show of force. But as is often the case in the Gospels, the disciples' vision was askew. Jesus had in mind a different kind of power, and a different mode of leadership. Jesus came as one who serves.

This story reminds me of a woman I met in Philadelphia. Laura and Samuel, our hosts while we were visiting the city to do mission work, introduced our group to Jolene. Jolene was an elderly woman, round in figure with graying hair, cane in hand to help her walk. She was a Christian. She invited us to join her in meeting members of the Philadelphia homeless community.

We provided sack lunches for all the people we met, learned their stories, and prayed for them.

Jolene's example was powerful. She befriended the homeless, met their needs, and provided social acceptance through warm conversation and kindly presence. She also recognized that the spiritual needs of the homeless needed to be addressed. She invited them to church so these new friends could connect with other disciples, receive and offer prayer, be encouraged, and experience the love of God.

Jolene came as a servant. She was following the model of Jesus. She prepared meals, made friends, and met needs, humbly in the name of Christ. Likewise, we are called to do simple acts of justice and mercy that meet tangible needs in our community, not for fame or glory or renown, but as servants.

God, you watch over the oppressed, the marginalized, the outcast, and the forgotten of our world. As your people, we are called to "get our hands dirty," engaging in the work of justice and mercy. Help me today to serve others in a Christ-like manner, offering kindness, compassion, and love. In Jesus's name. Amen.

38. USING OUR VOICES

Speak out on behalf of the voiceless, and for the rights of all who are vulnerable. Speak out in order to judge with righteousness and to defend the needy and the poor.
Proverbs 31:8-9

The story of Scripture carries many themes, but prominent among them is that of justice. Committed disciples serve God by doing justice, loving mercy, and walking humbly, as Micah 6:8 reminds us.

Author Shane Claiborne, a founding member of the new monastic community The Simple Way, describes the community in this manner: "We are trying to raise up an army not simply of street activists but lovers—a community of people who have fallen desperately in love with God and with suffering people, and who allow those relationships to disturb and transform them."[18]

This calling extends to all Christians. Service to God includes advocacy on behalf of those on the margins: the voiceless, the poor, the widow, and the orphan. I do not doubt you can bring others to mind who find themselves oppressed. The Bible is clear: Justice is found at the heart of God. Those who love God will do justice. And as we do justice among the voiceless and needy and vulnerable, we are changed.

Yet where to begin? Thomas à Kempis, a Medieval Catholic monk, wrote, "Do whatever lies in your power and God will assist your good intentions."[19] Do what you are able, with an attentive eye, watching closely for the works and movement of God.

Jesus commands us to provide clothing for those who have none, food for the hungry, drink for the thirsty, and comfort for those in prison. Doing justice encompasses all these tasks, and also takes many other forms. Talk to a pastor or other church leader. Find ministries in your city that are conducting work you are passionate about. Take to the streets, and love.

God, help me to serve others by doing justice. Our world is broken and in need of grace. Bring me into contact with those who are needy and poor and afflicted, and radiate your light through my life. May others see Christ in me as I work for what is right, speak up for those who are ignored, and advocate for those who are oppressed. May your will be done on earth as it is in heaven, in the doing and establishment of justice. In Jesus's holy name. Amen.

39. WORKING FOR PEACE

Whoever serves Christ in this way pleases God and gets human approval. So let's strive for the things that bring peace and the things that build each other up.

Romans 14:18-19

In my experience as a church leader, my greatest challenges came during times of great strain, those moments in ministry wherein, for whatever reason, people experienced a breakdown in relationship. Pain and anguish followed. Wise, patient leadership was required to help mediate the conflict and bring about a healthy resolution. I was not always successful. Whether you are a church leader or not, I expect you have experienced times of brokenness as well. What did you do? How did you handle the situation?

Our reading today gives us a clue. Romans 14 addresses a conflict. At Rome, some in the fellowship consumed meat sacrificed to idols. While some found no problem with this ("Idols do not exist! Why let the meat go to spoil?"), others took issue, thinking this was not proper for those in Christ. Disagreement ensued, and division followed. But Paul tells Christ's people at Rome to walk in love, to refrain from judging one another, and to live in "righteousness, peace, and joy in the Holy Spirit." According to Paul, all should act in accordance with their convictions concerning this matter.

As too many Christians can testify, fractures occur in our churches. Disagreements arise, and division comes shortly after. Some disagreements are healthy and are of critical importance. But others only concern trivial matters or questions of conscience without clear mandate from Scripture. In such matters, we should refrain from judgment, work for peace, and build one another up. In this way, we serve Christ by serving one another. Working through conflict in a loving and Christ-like way is a powerful testimony to the truth of the gospel.

Peacemaking "pleases God" and gains "human approval." Let us therefore serve God and neighbor by conducting our disagreements in love.

God, you have the power to heal deep wounds, to restore that which is broken, and to bring peace where there is division. Help me to be your agent in places of fissure, a bringer of salve for wounds that run deep. Serving Christ includes doing the things that make for peace, and speaking words that build up, rather than tear down. Help me to live in this posture, to your glory. In Christ's name. Amen.

40. GREATNESS OF
ANOTHER KIND

"Whoever wants to be great among you will be your servant."
Mark 10:43

We live in a world addicted to power and influence and fame. Christ calls us to another way. We are not to seek out fame and glory and greatness. We must humble ourselves and become servants.

In *The Great Divorce,* C. S. Lewis imaginatively explores the fruit of such a life. In Lewis's parable, a traveler from the fringes of hell visits the outskirts of heaven. There, he is able to witness both a hint of God's tremendous glory but also various failings and temptations that keep some from experiencing the fullness of God's presence.

Accompanied by a guide, the traveler witnesses a celebration of an indescribably majestic woman. "Is it? . . . Is it?" he whispers to his guide, attempting to discern who this might be.

> "Not at all," said he. "It's someone ye'll never have heard of. Her name on earth was Sarah Smith and she lived at Golders Green."
>
> "She seems to be . . . well, a person of particular importance?"
>
> "Aye. She is one of the great ones. Ye have heard that fame in this country and fame on Earth are two quite different things."[20]

Lewis captures the counterintuitive nature of Jesus' teaching: Greatness in God's eyes is attained in a different way. It is not those who dominate and "lord over" others who are to be exalted, but those who humble themselves, who take the path of descent, and serve. In Lewis's imaginative example, Ms. Smith is exalted for her love of children; even the animals that encountered her on the earth were enfolded within her love. And her love was not her own to give, but an extension of the love of Christ being poured forth through her life.

So too, when we serve others as ambassadors of Christ, we create space wherein the love of God might be revealed.

Go forth and serve, not to obtain your own glory but to make the glory of God manifest, inviting others to the eternal dance of his boundless love.

Lord Jesus, I understand that you came not to be served, but to serve, and to give your life to draw others unto yourself. Give me the grace to serve others. Amen.

TAKING A STEP

How can you better serve God and others today, even in small, commonplace tasks?

Resolve to live a life of service in the name of Jesus Christ.

Write down a few of your ideas, and prayerfully consider each one.

Then, choose one way that you can serve God, and act on your commitment.

NOTES

1. James Bryan Smith, *The Good and Beautiful Community: Following the Spirit, Extending Grace, Demonstrating Love* (Downers Grove, Illinois: IVP Books, 2010), 153.

2. Yushi Nomura and Henri Nouwen, *Desert Wisdom: Sayings From the Desert Fathers* (New York: Doubleday, 1982), 1.

3. Timothy Keller, *King's Cross: The Story of the World in the Life of Jesus* (New York: Dutton, 2011), University Press, 2006), 31.

4. Willard told this story at an informal "Dinner with Dallas" event at The United Methodist Church of the Resurrection (Leawood, KS) in January of 2006. I was in attendance at the event.

5. From W. H. Auden's "Herman Melville," as quoted in *The Yale Book of Quotations* (New Haven: Yale University Press, 2006), 31.

6. Sire, James. *Habits of the Mind: Intellectual Life as Christian Calling* (Downers Grove, IL: InterVarsity Press, 2000), pp. 178-79.

7. I heard Dr. Smith make this comment at Crossroads Community Church in Oklahoma City, Oklahoma at a 2009 Apprentice Conference event.

8. Stanley Hauerwas offers this observation in "The Insufficiency of Scripture: Why Discipleship is Required," *Unleashing the Scripture: Freeing the Bible from Captivity to America* (Nashville, TN: Abingdon Press, 1993), pp. 47-62.

9. Eugene H. Peterson, *Eat This Book: A Conversation in the Art of Spiritual Reading* (Grand Rapids, Michigan: William B. Eerdmans Publishing Company, 2006), 35.

10. C. S. Lewis, "Answers to Questions on Christianity," *The Collected*

Works of C.S. Lewis: God in the Dock (New York: Inspirational Press, 1996), 339.

11. Yushi Nomura, *Desert Wisdom: Sayings From the Desert Fathers* (New York: Doubleday, 1982), 106.

12. Alister McGrath, *Mere Apologetics: How to Help Seekers and Skeptics Find Faith* (Grand Rapids, Michigan: Baker Books, 2012), 22.

13. Stanley Hauerwas and William H. Willimon, *Resident Aliens: Life in the Christian Colony* (Nashville: Abingdon Press, 1989), 49.

14. William J. Abraham, *The Logic of Evangelism* (Grand Rapids, Michigan: William B. Eerdmans, 1989), 95.

15. Dallas Willard, *The Divine Conspiracy: Rediscovering Our Hidden Life in God* (San Francisco, HarperSanFrancisco, 1997), 329.

16. N. T. Wright, *The Challenge of Jesus: Rediscovering Who Jesus Was and Is,* (Downers Grove, Illinois: InterVarsity Press, 1999), 124.

17. Mother Teresa, *Everything Starts From Prayer: Mother Teresa's Meditations on Spiritual Life for People of All Faiths,* (Ashland, Oregon: White Cloud Press, 1998), 6.

18. Shane Claiborn, *The Irresitible Revolution: Living as an Ordinary Radical* (Grand Rapids, Michigan: Zondervan, 2006), 296.

19. Thomas a Kempis, *The Imitation of Christ* (New York: Vintage Books, 1998, 10.

20. C. S. Lewis, *The Great Divorce* (New York: Simon & Schuster, 1996), 105.